Hastamalakiyam

By Hastamalaka

Commentary by Adi Sankaracharya

Translation by Dr. H. Ramamoorthy and Nome

Published by
Society of Abidance in Truth (SAT)
1834 Ocean Street
Santa Cruz, CA 95060 USA
www.SATRamana.org
email: sat@cruzio.com

First Edition
ISBN: 9780981940991

Contents

Acknowledgements iv

Introduction v

Hastamalakiyam 1
A Fruit in the Hand or *A Work by Hastamalaka*

Attamalakam by Bhagavan Sri Ramana Maharshi 8

Hastamalakiya-Bhashyam by Adi Sankaracharya 12
Sri Sankara's Commentary on the Hymn of Hastamalaka

Acknowledgements

Deep appreciation and gratitude are here expressed for Raman Muthukrishnan and Sangeeta Raman for proofreading this book and distribution of SAT publications, for Raymond Teague and Ganesh Sadasivan for proofreading, for Richard Schneider for his generous donation making it possible to print this book and other SAT publications, for Sasvati for design and layout, and for all at the SAT Temple whose support of the temple and the publication of these teachings of Self-Knowledge has made the present book possible.

Introduction

This is a hymn that expounds Self-Knowledge and is addressed to Vishnu, the all-pervasive, the sustainer of the manifest world. It was composed by Hastamalaka, an immediate disciple of Adi Sankaracharya.

The accounts of Adi Sankara's life narrate that, during the Acharya's travels, he visited, one day, a village named Sri Bali, in the neighborhood of the shrine of Mukambika in south India. There, a Brahmana named Prabhakara brought his son, a boy of seven years, who, though handsome in appearance and gentle and patient in demeanor, was dumb and behaved like an idiot. He was made to prostrate before the Acharya. He did so but continued to remain in the prostrate position and refused to get up. The boy was lifted up by the Acharya.

The father said, "This boy is now seven years old, and his mind seems to be undeveloped. He has not even learned the alphabet, not to speak of the Vedas. Boys of his age come and call him for play, but he does not join them. Seeing him sitting silently, the boys beat him, but he does not show any sign of annoyance. Sometimes, he comes for food, and, sometimes, he abstains from all food. He does not heed any instruction. I have left it to his fate to direct his future."

The Acharya asked the boy, "Who are you? Why are you behaving in this manner, like an inert being?"

Questioned thus, the boy replied, "O, Great Teacher! I am not an inert thing. Even an inert thing becomes conscious in association with me. I am one with undivided Bliss. This Consciousness of the Atman is common to all liberated ones."

Then, in twelve verses, the boy expounded the Knowledge of the Self.

As Self-Knowledge was as natural and evident to him as an amalaka fruit in one's hand, he became famous under the name of "Hastamalaka." "Hastamalaka" is a phrase, or compound word, in Sanskrit idiom that denotes that which can be clearly, easily seen or understood. "Hasta" means hand, and "amalaka" is a small fruit with properties of rejuvenation, referred to botanically as the fruit of the emblic myrobalan.

The Acharya told the father, "This apparently dumb son of yours knows the truth of the Atman (the Self) by virtue of his practices in his past life. He must have inborn, intuitive knowledge. He does not have the least attachment to home and property; nor does he have any sense of 'I'-ness with regard to his body. How can one who knows all these objects, including the body, as external and unconnected with oneself, have any identification with them?"

So saying, Sri Sankara took this boy into his party and started toward the next destination.

The account regarding Hastamalaka is told in more detail by Madhava-Vidyaranya in *Sankara Digvijaya,* chapter 12, verses 38-62 (derived and adapted from the English translation by Swami Tapasyananda, Sri Ramakrishna Math):

For several days, the Acharya stayed at Mukambika, worshiping the Devi and receiving the reverential homage of many spiritual aspirants. He received and ate food obtained by holy begging (bhiksha). On one of those days, he, with his disciples, visited a village named Sri Bali, inhabited by about two thousand Brahmanas, where every house emitted the holy fragrance of the smoke of Agnihotra worship. The residents had abandoned all prohibited actions and spent all of their time in the study of the Vedas and in the performance of svadharma (one's own duties) and yajnas (act of worship or sacrifice). No untimely death ever occurred there. Located in that village was a temple in which was situated the murti (sanctified figure) of Lord Siva and His Consort in union, who looked like an ornament of gold studded with gems or like the sky with the disk of the moon.

Among the inhabitants of Sri Bali was one named Prabhakara. He was noted for his learning, his adherence to Vedic rites, and his life of holiness and beneficence. He had plenty of cattle, wealth, and relatives, but he was not happy because his only son was dumb and behaved like an idiot. Though the boy was handsome in appearance and very gentle and patient in demeanor, his behavior in other respects appeared like that of an idiot, hearing nothing, speaking nothing, and sitting alone in some corner in reverie. Prabhakara spent his days wondering if his son's behavior was due to possession, the result of past actions (karma), or merely the boy's nature. He anxiously awaited an opportunity to approach a wise man to learn the cause of his son's strange behavior,

Prabhakara heard that a great sage, accompanied by several disciples carrying some books, had come to the village. He decided to approach the Acharya with his son. Following the injunction that one should not visit with empty hands a deity or spiritual leader, Prabhakara approached Sri Sankara with a large offering of fruits and prostrated at his feet. His son, who shone like a fire-brand covered with ashes, was also made to prostrate before Sankara. The boy, though, remained in the prostrate position and refused to rise. The Acharya, in his infinite compassion, lifted him up. As the boy stood there, with his face looking downward, his father asked Sankara to enlighten him on the cause of the strange behavior of his son.

Prabhakara said, "He is now seven years old, and his mind seems to be undeveloped. He has not even learned the alphabet, not to mention the Vedas. The early period of his life has thus passed in vain. Boys of his age come and call him for play, but he does not join them. Seeing him sitting silently, the boys beat him, but he does not show any sign of annoyance. Sometimes, he comes for food, and, sometimes, he abstains from all food. He does not heed any instruction. I never try to rectify him by punishment but have left it to his fate to direct his future."

When the Brahmana finished his submission, the Acharya addressed the boy thus: "Who are you? Why are you thus behaving like an inert being?"

The boy replied, "O Great Teacher! Certainly, I am not an inert thing. Even an inert thing becomes conscious in association with me. I am one with undivided Bliss, free from the six states of suffering (sextet of anxieties), which are hunger, thirst, sorrow, despondence, old age, and death, and the sextet of states, which are origination, existence, growth, maturation, decay, and destruction. The Consciousness of the Self is the same for all of the liberated."

Then, in this manner, in twelve verses, he expounded the Knowledge of the Self. Because Self-Knowledge was naturally clearly evident to him, like an amalaka fruit in one's hand, he became well-known by the name Hastamalaka.

The primary text presented in this book is *Hastamalakiyam,* which means a work by or pertaining to Hastamalaka. It consists of twelve verses that succinctly reveal the Knowledge of the Self, proclaiming the identity of this eternal Knowledge and the Being of the Self. The term translated as "Knowledge," which appears in the fourth line of each of the first eleven verses, can also be interpreted as "Awareness," for Consciousness, itself, is the Knowledge that is eternal.

Also included in the present volume are an English translation of the Tamil version of the text by Bhagavan Sri Ramana Maharshi and an English translation of *Hastamalakiya-Bhashyam,* which is the Sanskrit commentary by Adi Sankara upon these verses by his disciple.

The following two verses appear in a *Sankara Vijayam,* a history of Sankara, and are the recounting by the author of a question posed by Sri Sankara to Hastamalaka and the latter's reply. These two verses are not part of a work composed by Sri Sankara or Hastamalaka. The *Hastamalakiyam,* or *Hastamalaka Stotram,* as it is sometimes referred to, as given by Hastamalaka starts after them. These verses, though, are included as introductory verses in Bhagavan Sri Ramana Maharshi's Tamil translation.

श्री शंकरः
śrī śaṅkaraḥ

कस्त्वं शिशो कस्य कुतोऽसि गन्ता
किं नाम ते त्वं कुत आगतोऽसि ।
एतन्मयोक्तं वद चार्भकस्त्वं
मत्प्रीतये प्रीतिविवर्धनोऽसि ॥

kas-tvaṁ śiśo kasya kuto'si gantā
kiṁ nāma te tvaṁ kuta āgato'si ।
etan-mayoktaṁ vada cārbhakas-tvaṁ
mat-prītaye prīti-vivardhano'si ।।

Sri Sankara [said]:

Who are you, oh child! Whose? Where are you going?
What is your name? From where have you come?
This is asked (said) by me. You, little boy, also tell,
For my satisfaction. You raise my affection.

हस्तामलकः

नाहं मनुष्यो न च देवयक्षौ
न ब्राह्मणक्षत्रियवैश्यशूद्राः ।
न ब्रह्मचारी न गृही वनस्थो
भिक्षुर्न चाहं निजबोधरूपः ॥

hastāmalakaḥ
nāhaṁ manuṣyo na ca deva-yakṣau
na brāhmaṇa-kṣatriya-vaiśya-śūdrāḥ ।
na brahmacārī na gṛhī vanastho
bhikṣur-na cāhaṁ nija-bodha-rūpaḥ ।।

Hastamalaka [said]:

I am not a man and not a god or yaksha (semi-divine being),
Not a brahmana (brahmin), warrior, trader, [or of the] servant class,
Not a brahmacari (student), not a householder, not a forest recluse,
And I am not a mendicant. I am of the nature of innate (constant, my own) Knowledge.

हस्तामलकीयम्
hastāmalakīyam

A Fruit in the Hand
or
A Work by Hastamalaka

निमित्तं मनश्चक्षुरादिप्रवृत्तौ
निरस्ताखिलोपाधिराकाशकल्पः ।
रविर्लोकचेष्टानिमित्तं यथा यः
स नित्योपलब्धिस्वरूपोऽहमात्मा ॥ १ ॥

nimittaṁ manaś-cakṣur-ādi-pravṛttau
nirastākhilopādhir-ākāśa-kalpaḥ ।
ravir-loka-ceṣṭā-nimittaṁ yathā yaḥ
sa nityopalabdhi-svarūpo'ham-ātmā ।। 1 ।।

The instrumental cause of the activity of the mind, eye, and others,
Devoid of all conditionings, akin to space,
Just as the sun is the instrumental cause of the world's activity,
That which by its nature is eternal Knowledge am I, the Self. (1)

यमग्न्युष्णवन्नित्यबोधस्वरूपं
मनश्चक्षुरादीन्यबोधात्मकानि ।
प्रवर्तन्त आश्रित्य निष्कम्पमेकं
स नित्योपलब्धिस्वरूपोऽहमात्मा ॥ २ ॥

yam-agny-uṣṇavan-nitya-bodha-svarūpam
manaś-cakṣur-ādīny-abodhātmakāni ।
pravartanta āśritya niṣkampam-ekaṁ
sa nityopalabdhi-svarūpo'ham-ātmā ।। 2 ।।

Resorting to that which is of the nature that is eternal and is Knowledge,
The mind, eye, and others not possessed of Knowledge, enter into activity,
Like fire and heat, the unwavering One,
That which by its nature is eternal Knowledge am I, the Self. (2)

मुखाभासको दर्पणे दृश्यमानो
मुखत्वात्पृथक्त्वेन नैवास्ति वस्तु ।
चिदाभासको धीषु जीवोऽपि तद्वत्
स नित्योपलब्धिस्वरूपोऽहमात्मा ॥ ३ ॥

mukhābhāsako darpaṇe dṛśyamāno
mukhatvāt-pṛthaktvena naivāsti vastu ।
cid-ābhāsako dhīṣu jīvo'pi tadvat-
sa nityopalabdhi-svarūpo'ham-ātmā ।। 3 ।।

The reflection of the face seen in a mirror
Is not a thing that exists different from the nature of the face;
The reflection of Consciousness in the minds, the individual self, is also like that;
That which by its nature is eternal Knowledge am I, the Self. (3)

यथा दर्पणाभाव आभासहानौ
मुखं विद्यते कल्पनाहीनमेकम् ।
तथा धीवियोगे निराभासको यः
स नित्योपलब्धिस्वरूपोऽहमात्मा ॥ ४ ॥

yathā darpaṇābhāva ābhāsa-hānau
mukhaṁ vidyate kalpanā-hīnam-ekam ।
tathā dhī-viyoge nir-ābhāsako yaḥ
sa nityopalabdhi-svarūpo'ham-ātmā ।। 4 ।।

Just as in the absence of the mirror, [with] the disappearance of the reflection,
The face, without being imagined, remains one,
So, likewise, on separation from the mind, that which remains as the non-reflected (or, without a reflection),
That which by its nature is eternal Knowledge am I, the Self. (4)

मनश्चक्षुरादेर्वियुक्तः स्वयं यो
मनश्चक्षुरादेर्मनश्चक्षुरादिः ।
मनश्चक्षुरादेरगम्यस्वरूपः
स नित्योपलब्धिस्वरूपोऽहमात्मा ॥ ५ ॥

manaś-cakṣur-āder-viyuktaḥ svayaṁ yo
manaś-cakṣur-āder-manaś-cakṣur-ādiḥ ।
manaś-cakṣur-āder-agamya-svarūpaḥ
sa nityopalabdhi-svarūpo'ham-ātmā ।। 5 ।।

Separated from the mind, eye, and others, that which, by itself,
Is the Mind, Eye, and Others of the mind, eye, and others,
And is of a nature beyond the reach of the mind, eye, and others,
That which by its nature is eternal Knowledge am I, the Self. (5)

य एको विभाति स्वतः शुद्धचेताः
प्रकाशस्वरूपोऽपि नानेव धीषु ।
शरावोदकस्थो यथा भानुरेकः
स नित्योपलब्धिस्वरूपोऽहमात्मा ॥ ६ ॥

ya eko vibhāti svataḥ śuddha-cetāḥ
prakāśa-svarūpo'pi nāneva dhīṣu ।
śarāvodakastho yathā bhānur-ekaḥ
sa nityopalabdhi-svarūpo'ham-ātmā ।। 6 ।।

That which, being One, the pure Consciousness, though of the nature of the self-luminous,
Shines as if variegated in the minds,
Just as the sun, being one, existing in water in platters,
That which by its nature is eternal Knowledge am I, the Self. (6)

यथानेकचक्षुःप्रकाशो रविर्न
क्रमेण प्रकाशीकरोति प्रकाश्यम् ।
अनेका धियो यस्तथैकप्रबोधः
स नित्योपलब्धिस्वरूपोऽहमात्मा ॥ ७ ॥

yathāneka-cakṣuḥ-prakāśo ravir-na
krameṇa prakāśī-karoti prakāśyam ।
anekā dhiyo yas-tathaika-prabodhaḥ
sa nityopalabdhi-svarūpo'ham-ātmā ।। 7 ।।

Just as the sun, illumining numerous eyes,
Does not illumine sequentially what is to be illumined,
So it is with that which, being One, is the awakener of numerous minds simultaneously,
That which by its nature is eternal Knowledge am I, the Self. (7)

विवस्वत्प्रभातं यथारूपमक्षं
प्रगृह्णाति नाभातमेवं विवस्वान् ।
यदाभात आभासयत्यक्षमेकः
स नित्योपलब्धिस्वरूपोऽहमात्मा ॥ ८ ॥

vivasvat-prabhātaṁ yathā-rūpam-akṣaṁ
pragṛhṇāti nābhātam-evaṁ vivasvān |
yad-ābhāta ābhāsayaty-akṣam-ekaḥ
sa nityopalabdhi-svarūpo'ham-ātmā || 8 ||

Just as, illumined by the sun, the eye recognizes the form not illumined,
So, likewise, the One, illumined by which
The sun illumines the eye;
That which by its nature is eternal Knowledge am I, the Self. (8)

यथा सूर्य एकोऽप्स्वनेकश्चलासु
स्थिरास्वप्यनन्वग्विभाव्यस्वरूपः ।
चलासु प्रभिन्नासु धीष्वेवमेकः
स नित्योपलब्धिस्वरूपोऽहमात्मा ॥ ९ ॥

yathā sūrya eko'psvanekaś-calāsu
sthirāsvapy-ananvag-vibhāvya-svarūpaḥ |
calāsu prabhinnāsu dhīṣvevam-ekaḥ
sa nityopalabdhi-svarūpo'ham-ātmā || 9 ||

Just as the sun, the one, in many waters moving and stationary,
Is to be looked upon as of a nature not following,
Though only One, seen as many in moving minds,
That which by its nature is eternal Knowledge am I, the Self. (9)

घनच्छन्नदृष्टिर्घनच्छन्नमर्कं
यथा निष्प्रभं मन्यते चातिमूढः।
तथा बद्धवद्भाति यो मूढदृष्टेः
स नित्योपलब्धिस्वरूपोऽहमात्मा ॥ १० ॥

ghanacchanna-dṛṣṭir-ghanacchannam-arkam
yathā niṣprabhaṁ manyate cātimūḍhaḥ |
tathā baddhavad-bhāti yo mūḍha-dṛṣṭeḥ
sa nityopalabdhi-svarūpo'ham-ātmā || 10 ||

Just as a great fool with his vision obscured by the clouds
Thinks that the sun obscured by the clouds is not shining,
Likewise, that which seems to be bound to the perception of the ignorant,
That which by its nature is eternal Knowledge am I, the Self. (10)

समस्तेषु वस्तुष्वनुस्यूतमेकं
समस्तानि वस्तूनि यं न स्पृशन्ति।
वियद्वत्सदा शुद्धमच्छस्वरूपः
स नित्योपलब्धिस्वरूपोऽहमात्मा ॥ ११ ॥

samasteṣu vastuṣvanusyūtam-ekaṁ
samastāni vastūni yaṁ na spṛśanti |
viyadvat-sadā śuddham-accha-svarūpaḥ
sa nityopalabdhi-svarūpo'ham-ātmā || 11 ||

Woven together in all manifest things, the One,
Whom all manifest things do not touch,
Of a nature ever pure and transparent like space,
That which by its nature is eternal Knowledge am I, the Self. (11)

उपाधौ यथा भेदता सन्मणीनां
तथा भेदता बुद्धिभेदेषु तेऽपि ।
यथा चन्द्रिकाणां जले चञ्चलत्वं
तथा चञ्चलत्वं तवापीह विष्णो ॥ १२ ॥

upādhau yathā bhedatā sanmaṇīnāṁ
tathā bhedatā buddhi-bhedeṣu te'pi |
yathā candrikāṇāṁ jale cañcalatvaṁ
tathā cañcalatvaṁ tavāpīha viṣṇo || 12 ||

Just as there is difference for pure crystals due to conditioning (apparent limitation, appearance of another thing),
Likewise there is difference for you in different intellects;
Just as for moons in waters, there is movement to and fro,
Likewise is there movement for you also here (in minds), O All-pervasive One (Vishnu) (12)

Attamalakam

by

Bhagavan Sri Ramana Maharshi

When Sri Jagadguru Sankara was touring the west coast of India, a brahmin named Prabhakar, who resided there in the village of Srivali, came to know of the Acharya's visit. He took his thirteen-year-old son, prostrated in the presence of the Guru, stood up, and made his son also prostrate. He then narrated the history of his son, who was mute from birth and who was devoid of interest in any activity, desire or aversion, and honor or dishonor. Upon hearing this, the Master lifted the boy in his arms and, full of joy, asked him thus:

O Child! (O Boy!) You who have come here (to this state), who
 are you? Whose son are you (Who is the cause of
 your birth)?
Whither are you bound (What is the goal of your birth)?
What is your name? Wherefrom have you come (Wherefrom
 have you reached this body)?
Speak to gladden my heart! Sankara asking thus, the boy
 opened his mouth and [began] to speak (reply). (1)

I am not a man, I am not a god, and not a yaksha (a semi-
 divine being).
I am not a brahmin or any others, such as a king, trader, or [of
 the] servant class.
I am not a good brahmacari (student of the Vedas), a householder, a recluse in the forest (vanaprasta), or a blemishless
 sannyasin (renouncer)—not anyone of this group.
I am of the nature of Reality (Truth) and Knowledge. (2)

Just as the sun is said to be the cause for the activities in
the world,
He who is the cause of all the activities of the mind, eye,
and others,
He who is like space, devoid of all conditionings,
Who remains as the nature that is One, who is eternal [and] is
Consciousness (eternal Consciousness), that Self am I. (3)

Just like fire and its heat, He who is of the nature of the eternal
and Knowledge (eternal Knowledge),
Being One, motionless, and illuminating,
Resorting to whom the insentient (devoid of Knowledge) organs
of action, senses, and such enter into their own (respective)
activities,
Of the nature of Knowledge, eternal Consciousness, that Self
am I. (4)

The face reflected in the mirror is not another thing apart from
the face.
Likewise, arising as the reflection of Consciousness in the
intellect is the jiva (the individual self).
He who is not in the least anything different from the nature of
Consciousness,
[The one] without a second, eternal Consciousness, that Self
am I. (5)

If the mirror, itself, is not there, there is not the reflection of
the face.
What remains as the object, itself, is the one face only, devoid
of modification.
He who shines [when] the intellect disappears,
Of that nature, eternal Consciousness, that Self am I. (6)

He who is not connected with the mind, eye, and others,
He who is the Mind, Eye, and Others for the mind, eye,
and others,
He who is not touched by the mind, eye, and others,
He who is not transient, is eternal, and exists as Consciousness,
that Self am I. (7)

The sun appearing in the waters in various pots is only one.
Likewise, though shining as variegated in various intellects
(every intellect) in the bodies, the One shines by Himself,
Pure, as Consciousness, not to be attained anew.
He who is eternal and exists as Consciousness,
that Self am I. (8)

The one luminous sun illumines the world simultaneously for
numerous eyes.
Likewise, the One, of the nature of Knowledge, being the Light,
Illumines this world for numerous intellects.
Limitless, eternal, and existing as Consciousness,
that Self am I. (9)

The eye illumined by the sun alone perceives the form existing
in front;
Not illumined by the sun, it cannot.
Likewise, the One by whose Light the sun, itself, illumines the
eye and others,
Formless, eternal Consciousness, that Self am I. (10)

The one sun appears like the many in moving waters.
In water devoid of movement, it, itself, appears as only one.
Though appearing in moving intellects as if many,
The One, he who is motionless, eternal Consciousness, that
Self am I. (11)

Like a great fool, because of his vision (lit., eyes) being
obstructed by the clouds,
Thinking that the sun has become devoid of light,
He who, in the ignorant man's vision, looks like one completely
covered,
He who is motionless, eternal Consciousness, that Self
am I. (12)

Being One, woven through (in) all things, yet to (in) all
things unattached,
He who is like space, ever pure, and blemishless,
He who is of the nature of the egoless (devoid of "I"),
Eternal, existing as Consciousness, that Self am I. (13)

The [transparent] crystal will appear in various ways (colors) by
various conditionings,
So, also, for you, in various ways, in various intellects;
Like the movement of the moon in reflections due to
movement in waters,
There will be movement in the moving (unsteady) intellects for
you also, O perfectly full One! (14)

Because of revealing the Self, like a berry (amalaka) in the hand
(palm),
This [hymn] became known by the name of *Attamalaka
Tottiram (Hastamalaka Stotra);*
Besides, thus, that boy, great in wisdom,
Was extolled in this world by all as Hastamalaka.
How wondrous!

The Acharya told the father, who was beside himself in wonder, "It is your good fortune that he has become your son due to the unfulfilled tapas of the past. There will be no use for you in this life from him. Let him be with me." Saying thus, the Acarya sent the parent away and took the boy with him.

Later, the disciples asked the Guru, "What is the cause of this boy being established in Brahman without any prior sadhana (spiritual practice) like sravana (listening) and such?"

The Guru told them, "Once, his mother left the two-year-old child with a sadhu (holy man), who was a siddha-yogi (accomplished yogi) who possessed all powers, while she went to bathe along with the other ladies in the Yamuna River. The child slowly walked away, fell into the river, and died. To assuage the anguish of the mother at the loss, the sadhu left his body and entered the body of the child. Hence, his greatness.

Hastamalakiya-Bhashyam

by Adi Sankaracharya

Sri Sankara's Commentary on the Hymn of Hastamalaka

Knowing which all shall be discerned
As being in the Supreme Self,
To that Eternal-Knowledge-Bliss,
Originless and changeless, I bow (I worship).

By ignorance of which duality came into being
(appears),
On knowing which, it disappears (ceases),
Like the rope-serpent, completely (absolutely),
To that Supreme Spirit (or: the best of men), I bow
(I worship).

By the knowledge of whose teachings,
(By the devoted spiritual reflection upon whose
spiritual teachings),
Our Consciousness-Self shines (becomes evident),
To that Sadguru, the sun,
That dispels the darkness of one's own ignorance,
I bow (I offer salutations).

Here, certainly, for all living beings, by one's own natural inclination, indeed, there is the wish to accept happiness and the desire to abandon suffering, thus—"Let there be happiness for me; let there not be suffering for me."

In this context, someone who possesses full, superior, abundant merit, having known that suffering is inevitable and that happiness born of sense objects is without reality, is impermanent, and is, thus, suffering, indeed, by striving with aspiration, by spiritual practice, and by perfect, very strong abandonment of attachment to samsara, is free from passion.

With indifference to and having no interest in attachment, he endeavors to reach the relinquishment of samsara. (or: With indifference and relinquishment of samsara, he strives.)

As non-knowledge, or misunderstanding, of the true nature of the Self and turning away from Self-Knowledge are [the cause and production] of samsara, the Acharya (spiritual teacher) instructs him in the Knowledge of the Self.

The instrumental cause of the activity of the mind, eye, and others,
Devoid of all conditionings, akin to space,
Just as the sun is the instrumental cause of the world's activity,
That which by its nature is eternal Knowledge am I, the Self. (1)

Is it not that always, at the beginning of a text, there is first conceived and brought forth the praise of and offering of homage to the chosen, worshiped deity of the wise author (lit., of the wise men)?

In the absence of this respectful praise and offering of homage by the author, may there thus be applicable any expression of unrefined, unwise, disrespectful, or neglectful behavior? If this is the view, no.

This is because praise and offering of homage exist as threefold. There are, thus, the threefold praise and offering of homage in the body, in speech, and in the mind.

Therefore, though, even in the absence of those of the body and speech, because of the supreme wisdom of the teacher and the conclusion (completion), without obstacle, of the text, it is to be thus understood that this teacher praised and offered homage with the mind.

Let this be. We shall follow the orignal subject of discussion under consideration.

"Mind" (manaḥ) and "eye" (cakṣuḥ) are "mind-and-eye"; both of these "and others" compound to form "mind, eye, and others" (manaścakṣurādīni). The word "and others" (ādi) connects (compounds) with each one.

From there, this meaning of "of the mind and others," becomes of the mind (manaḥ), the ego (ahaṅkāra), the intellect (buddhi), thought (memory, citta), which are the four inner senses (i.e., the four aspects of the mind). So, also, "of the eye and others," means the eye, the skin, the ear, the tongue, the nose, which are the five senses (sense organs) of perception, and speech, hand, foot, organ of excretion (anus), and the generative organ, which are the five organs of action.

"In activity" (pravṛttau "of the activity," "in coming forth") means engagement in one's own activity. "The instrumental cause" (nimittaṁ) means that which is the cause (hetuḥ, reason). That am I, the Self (so'ham-ātmā); thus is the connection.

It is of what kind? Thus, it is desirable and expected that he said, "Eternal Knowledge (nityopalabdhiḥ)." Eternal (nityā) and that Knowledge (upalabdhiḥ), also, are thus "eternal Knowledge" (nityopalabdhiḥ). That which is such of its own nature, therefore, is that which is proclaimed.

The "sun" (raviḥ) is the sun (ādityaḥ), the celestial luminary. "In which manner" (yathā) is by which way, by its luminescence. "In the activities of the worlds" (lokānāṁ ceṣṭāyāṁ), it is "the cause" (nimittaṁ), the cause (hetuḥ, the reason), that vibrates, or flashes forth, and is in motion. Likewise, indeed, by being the governing power, which is the cause (nimittaṁ), "That am I, the Self," is the meaning, the truth. Thus, this view has been revealed as the approach to Self-Knowledge.

From the Supreme Truth shall be "removed" (nirasta), rejected (nirākṛtāḥ), "all" (akhilāḥ), without remainder or exception (niravaśeṣāḥ), all limitations (conditionings, suppositions, disguises) (upādhayaḥ), such as the characteristics of the intellect and others. Therefore, of that it is said, "devoid of all conditionings" (nirastākhilopādhiḥ). It is because of being devoid of all conditionings, indeed, that this is "akin to space" (ākāśakalpaḥ), which means completely pure like space. Thus is the meaning and the truth.

Is it not, in the progression (entrance) into the activities of the mind, eye, and others, that dependence on, or being governed by, something is acknowledged or expected? Why do they not issue forth and act of their own? Also, how is "being of the nature of eternal Knowledge" (nityopalabdhisvarūpatvam) acknowledged (regarded) as the governing power? Thus, going forward, he declares:

Resorting to that which is of the nature that is eternal and is Knowledge,
The mind, eye, and others not possessed of Knowledge, enter into activity,
Like fire and heat, the unwavering One,
That which by its nature is eternal Knowledge am I, the Self. (2)

Dependent on the true nature of the Self, which is eternal Knowledge, the mind, the eye and others enter activity; that is I, the Self. Thus is the connection.

Indeed, what is the eternality of Knowledge?

Knowledge (bodhaḥ or understanding, awareness) is, indeed, named knowledge (jñānam), and that is generated and brought forth by the connection, or drawing together, of the senses, the objects, and others. The knowledge arisen, which is mentioned, by its own function of accomplishment or by exclusion, or prevention, and removal by interior knowledge, utterly disappears and is destroyed. Hence, because of its character, or properties, of origin and destruction, it does not deserve to be considered as eternal. Nor, still, does the knowledge (bodhaḥ) approach the true nature of the Self, because of the eternality of the Self and the non-eternality of the knowledge. Nor, certainly, can eternality and non-eternality pertain to one and the same innate nature, because of contradiction.

Then, it is said, indeed, by the term "knowledge" (bodhaḥ), sentience (caitanyam, intelligence, consciousness) is meant. Knowledge (jñānam) is also not sentience (caitanyam), which is the knowledge produced with the to-be-known, or the perceived, like pots and such that are inert.

The to-be-known, indeed, is Knowledge (jñānam), as the knowledge of the pot is brought into existence for, and is apparent to, me (i.e., it is my pot-knowledge), and the knowledge of the cloth is brought into existence for, and is apparent to, me (i.e., it is my cloth-knowledge). This is what is actually, evidently, being experienced.

Hence, with the non-eternality of that and the not being the true nature of the Self, also, the Self being of the true nature of eternal Knowledge (bodhaḥ) is arrived at.

Surely, if [it is asked], "What is the proof of the Consciousness (cetanatve) of the Self?" we shall say, "The shining (manifestation) of the universe."

"The universe is manifested (is illumined)" is established as the settled conclusion of all people. Therefore, by the knowledge and such and with the to-be-known-ness being inert, that it is by the shining light of the Self alone that the universe shines (is manifested), it is ascertained and becomes certain.

Also, the Self is self-luminous, being the light for oneself and others, like the luminous sun. Just as the sun, by itself being luminous, illumines the world, so does the Self likewise.

Let it be, then, that the Spirit (purusha) has Consciousness as a dharma (nature, character, property, essential quality). (or: Let it be, then, that the Spirit is the Consciousness-nature.) How is this the innate nature of Consciousness?

No, because of the inapplicability and incompatibility of the existence of the quality (character, dharma) and the one who has the quality (dharmi).

Thus, surely, sentience (caitanyam, consciousness) is different, non-different, or both-different-and-nondifferent from the Self.

In that case, therefore, it is not of such difference. If different, like a pot, it is incompatible with and inapplicable to the nature (dharma) of the Self.

The pot is certainly not at all related to and has no connection with the nature of the Self. (or: The pot does not at all become a quality or characteristic of the Self.) [If the view is,] "Sentience (consciousness, caitanya), though, is connected with the Self, thus joined as a quality (dharmatvam) of the Self," still no, for connection is incompatible and inapplicable.

Connection is, indeed, so long as contact (conjunction, union) (saṁyogaḥ) or combination (perpetual co-inherence, inseparable concomitance, constant and intimate relation or union) (samavāyaḥ) may be. Another type of connection is not possible and is nonexistent here.

It is not possibly saṁyogaḥ (conjunction, union), because that is a property (quality, dharma) only of material objects or substances. Sentience (consciousness, caitanya) is not an object or material thing.

It is also not samavāyaḥ (combination, perpetual co-inherence, inseparable concomitance, constant and intimate relation or union) because of non-finality and an endless series of statements.

samavāyaḥ (combination, perpetual co-inherence, inseparable concomitance, constant and intimate relation or union) is certainly binding together or connected (sambaddhaḥ). It binds together the united constituents or concomitant partners; or are they not bound?

It is, perhaps, just unbound and not connected, as in the case of pots and such, in which the connection is not made of anything.

With the nonexistence of the connection (saṁyogaḥ) and such, though, some samavāyaḥ (combination, perpetual co-inherence, inseparable concomitance, constant and intimate relation or union) other than samavāyaḥ (or, another samavāyaḥ) is to be inferred and agreed upon.

Thus, because of the consideration of the series, or succession, (or, Thus, because of the dependent series) there is the becoming apparent of and descending into non-finality, the unsettledness of an endless series of propositions. Thus, let this be.

Therefore, from the perspective of difference (being different), the supposition of the existence of the quality (dharma) and the possessor of the quality (dharmi), in every respect, is not arrived at or partaken of.

But from the perspective of non-difference, indeed, with the nature of the Self being of the knowledge, still more, the existence, or supposition, of the quality (dharma) and the possessor of the quality (dharmi) does not exist at all, indeed.

Certainly, That, itself, does not become a quality of That; white (whiteness) certainly does not become a quality of white, thus.

Therefore, the perspective of being different-and-not-different alone remains. That, also, is inconsistent and incongruous because it is not homogeneous and is self-contradictory; certainly, the One is not able to be both different and not different from the One, due to there being inconsistency, incongruence, and antithesis.

Here, it may be said, "Because it is established in direct experience, difference-and-nondifference is not contradictory.

"So, indeed, 'This is a cow': by this unerring, non-exclusive distinction of a body, a lump of flesh, cowness is recognized. That, alone, in another body, which is the same conception understood with difference, is recognized or conceived. Hence, by direct experience (direct perception), indeed, difference-and non-difference is the confirmed conception and opinion and is not contradictory."

We consider this as incorrect. The establishment of direct experience (direct perception) is otherwise. (or: What is established is otherwise than what is of direct perception.) Though, indeed, different, a thing, by direct perception, is conceived and considered as non-different, because of the detrimental effect (fault) of complete (i.e., immediate) proximity and such. Just as the flames of a light (lamp), though different or divided, due to any reason, appear as non-different and undivided, just so, though non-different and undivided, a thing, or the reality, appears as if different and divided. It is just as, from the one moon, a second moon appears. For this reason, that the establishment of direct perception is otherwise, (or: For this reason of what is established is otherwise than what is of direct perception,) by that direct perception there is not establishment of proof, and the rejection and repudiation of the contradictory and inconsistent different-and-not-different concept is appropriate.

Now, it may be said, "Sentience (consciousness, caitanya) is in two forms (i.e., there are two forms of caitanya): being the true nature of the Self and being the own nature of sentience (consciousness). Therein, being the true nature of the Self is not different or split from the Self and is different or split as the own nature or form of sentience (caitanya). Hence, because of both forms, being different-and-non-different is not incompatible or inconsistent."

That is also not so, because of the nonexistence of quality (dharma) and possessor of the quality (dharmi).

Therefore, indeed, by which nature that is non-different, by that nature it is not its quality, because of being non-different, we have said.

By which nature it is different, by (because of) that, also, it is not its quality, because being different like pots and such. Thus it is declared.

That which has been said, that by both forms there is difference-and-non-difference, that, also, does not withstand inquiry.

Are both these in a form different, non-different, or different-and-non-different from sentience (caitanya)?

Therein, in that case, it is not in a different nature, in difference like pots and such, and the difference is made of nothing whatsoever. Thus, in non-difference only is sentience (caitanya), indeed. There is not both difference-and-non-difference.

Because of contradiction and incompatibility, difference-and-non-difference, indeed, also are not united and is not appropriate.

The inner nature or different form of these two, though, again leads to difference-and-non-difference-ness, which approaches an endless non-finality. Thus, enough with much expatiation.

Therefore, the Self is not at all a quality (dharma) of Consciousness (cit). Then, what?

It is thus, indeed, the true nature (own nature) of Consciousness.

In this way, the true nature of the Self has been expounded even to Sadananda.

The Self is eternal, also, having no real cause, like an infinitesimal particle. Being the Self, it is recognized and understood by itself as "I am."

It is also causeless. It does not, indeed, belong to, and is not derived from, a cause, as a thing perceptible by direct perception and such, and is also not heard of being so.

But, being the one cause of the three worlds, of the Self it is certainly heard, "From That (Brahman), indeed, from this Self, space came into being," and such from the Vedas.

There is certainly not any other cause of the Self.

Therefore, because there is no real cause, the Self is eternal. Thus it is established.

Therefore, it is rightly declared, "the true nature is eternal Knowledge."

There, indeed, an example is thus given: "like fire and heat," just as being hot, or the property of heat, is not separated from fire.

For separation, or difference, would be if, at any time, fire were otherwise perceived, just as a staff and such from a man, and it is not like this. Therefore, the nature of fire, itself, is being of the heat of fire and is the property of fire's heat.

Thus, for (lit., of) the Self, also, sentience (caitanya) is its own nature (svarūpam), indeed. Thus is the meaning.

Accordingly, it is declared, "Being partless and being all-pervasive and omnipresent, likewise being the imperishable existence, in both Brahman and space, there is no difference; sentience is the abundance of Brahman (or, subsequent to Brahman)."

Also, that which has been said about the mind, eye, and others in activity and coming forth, "Why is a ruler or governing power required and to be accepted? Why is it not that by themselves alone they start acting?" There it is declared, "They are non-knowing, non-perceptive, in themselves."

This distinguishing attribute, or distinction, is cause-containing, or cause-related. Hence, also, this meaning arises (setsyati): "Because of being without knowledge (non-perceptive) in themselves, and being non-Consciousness (insentient, non-comprehending), like a pot and others, they are, indeed, dependent on (resort to) the governing power of Consciousness to become active."

That insentience (non-Consciousness) and the sought are that "being known" like a pot and others, thus.

The Sruti (Vedas), also, [by stating], "Therefore, there is no other seer," and such, negate and deny a consciousnesss (sentience) different from the Self.

Hence, it is rightly declared, "Dependent on the Self that is Consciousness, they become active," thus.

Motionless (niṣkampaṁ) is unwavering, without waves, and without doubt. Thus is the meaning.

So, too, the Sruti (Vedas) says, "The knot of the heart is untied, cut asunder, all doubts are effaced (cut off), and [all one's] karmas (actions) are dissipated and perish, when that which is both the high and the low, the all-inclusive, is known (seen)."

The One (ekam) is without a second; it is the One in the bodies of gods, animals, human beings, and others, but not as manifold or differently as is imagined in sāṅkhya and others. This is the meaning.

"Is it not that in the Self being One, there will be states of happiness, sorrow, and such? Just so, indeed, for, if there shall be one Self in all bodies, then, in one's happiness (when one person is happy), all, indeed, will be provided with happiness, because of all being non-different and not distinct. Thus, in one's sorrow (if one person is in sorrow), all, indeed, will be in sorrow. Thus, if one person knows, all, indeed, will know. So, indeed, in one person being born or dying, all, indeed, should be born or be dead. Thus, if one person is bound or is liberated, all, indeed, shall be bound or liberated, thus.

"And it is not so. Therefore, the Self does not qualify, and is not able, to be Oneness."

So, it is further said:

The reflection of the face seen in a mirror
Is not a thing that exists different from the nature of the face;
The reflection of Consciousness in the minds, the individual self (jiva), is also like that;
That which by its nature is eternal Knowledge am I, the Self. (3)

The "reflection of the face (mukhābhāsakaḥ)" is the reflected image of a face (mukhapratibimbaḥ); "in a mirror" and such is in mirrors of various forms; Likewise is "being seen from the face (mukhatvāt)," truly speaking, really is from the own form or nature of the face (mukhasvarūpatvāt); "by being apart (pṛthaktvena)" is by being different, and that does not exist.

If, though, the reflection is really not a real thing, indeed, and is only an appearance and not, indeed, a reality, still, though, because of the difference in conditionings (limitations, defining attributes, a substitute having the mere name or appearance of the other thing) and the truly existent face, one from another, they, the reflections of the face, appear as different.

So, also, because of the qualities of dirtiness, or being tarnished, and such contained in the conditionings, or limitations, the qualities of dirtiness and such appear [in the reflections].

"Like that" is like the reflection of the face; "the reflection of Consciousness," is the reflection of the Self in the intelligences, in the intellects, seen in the mind, and that which is thus said to be a jiva (individual being). That "I" is the Self. Those jivas (individual beings), because of the difference of conditionings, or limitations, appear as different.

Because of the happiness, sorrow, and such being contained in the conditionings or limitations, they are reflected as having happiness, sorrow, and such within.

The conditionings, or limitations, are, also, of the form of being determined with fixed limits and respective differences, indeed, and thus of the happiness, sorrow, and such. Thus, the established conviction of the Oneness of the Self is established as alone right, and the difference of this Self is not possible to be established.

The Sruti (Vedas), also, set forth the Oneness of the Self thus, "Brahman is One only, without a second."

From the supposition, or viewpoint, of difference in and of the Self, though, this condition or state of happiness, sorrow, and such should not be produced.

So, indeed, "differences pertaining to the body are of the Self, and they are in all as they pertain to one, being all-pervasive," thus the adherents to the doctrine of difference in or of the Self (i.e., a multiplicity of selves) opine.

In that case, if in all of them there is all-pervasiveness, in the presence of all, there is the nonexistence, or absence, of any distinct, particular cause to generate happiness and such; how there can be the happiness and such of one alone and not in all of them, thus, is possible to be ascertained.

Now, that connected with which there is the combination (striking together) of cause and effect, or a particular cause, so that happiness and such are generated, of that alone that may thus be considered; this is not so. Though there is the combination of the cause and effect, in the presence of all the selves, because of the nonexistence, or absence, of a particular, distinct cause being generated, indeed, how can there thus be a connection to one self?

Now, if it is thought, "The action (karma) dependent upon which and in consequence of which the combination of cause and effect arises, for that alone is that combination of cause and effect, and there is the particular cause or reason,"

No, because of the action, also, in the presence of all of the selves, being generated with connection to all of the selves, that being produced by, or born of, the cause and effect combination, also, being connected with all of the selves, of that produced happiness, sorrow, and such, there is also the connection with all of the selves of happiness and such. The different, various selves supposition thus is not established.

There is also the fault of the non-finality of an endless series in the consideration of the karma of each previous combination of cause and effect.

By being originless (beginningless), also, the removal, or remedying, of the fault of the non-finality of an endless series is the darkness and blindness of an uninterrupted succession (i.e., an endless regression), thus.

The Sruti (Vedas), also, denies the supposition of a variety of different selves thus, "Not here is difference at all."

Hence, it is correctly declared by the holy, "One." ("It is One.")

Is it not that, because of the nonexistence of the Self's connection with happiness, sorrow, and such, bondage is not? Because of the nonexistence of bondage, there is the nonexistence of liberation. The bound, certainly, may be liberated, not the unbound. Just so, also, of the reflection of Consciousness, bondage and liberation do not exist. Because of that intellect's destructibility, also, there is the nonexistence of bondage and liberation. Consequently, also, [the idea,] "the liberation teaching is meaningless, worthless nonsense," is obtained. Hence, it is further said (literally, an untranslatable interjection signifying reproof or emphasis),

Just as in the absence of the mirror, [with] the
disappearance of the reflection,
The face, without being imagined, remains one,
So, likewise, on separation from the mind, that which
remains as the non-reflected (or, without a reflection),
That which by its nature is eternal Knowledge am I,
the Self. (4)

"Just as in the absence, or nonexistence, of the mirror," which is the being of the reflection, "upon the disappearance of the reflected" face, there is the real "face," the existence of the real thing, "without imagination," free from false knowledge, "the one" alone, the beyond and final, not another and not different, exists, "so, likewise," by that, indeed, in that manner, "upon separation from the mind," in the nonexistence of the intellect, "without a reflection," the absence of the reflected, being the real thing, the supreme Truth, there is that which is only one. That "I" is the Self. Thus is it to be connected; this is the application of the sense of the passage.

This is the approach and the aim. Ignorance of the Self made, resulted in, this intellect and such and the manifested universe.

Therein, by the form of the reflection in the intellect and such, that which is superimposed on the Self throws, or imposes, what is directed toward happiness, sorrow, and such upon the Self.

It is this imposition, or influence, that is bondage.

By Self-Knowledge, there is reversion from, an escape from, ignorance, and in the reversion, or turning back, from the intellect and others and the manifested universe, and the reversion from the imposition, is liberation.

Not, again, in the supreme Truth do bondage and liberation exist; thus, all is correct and consistent.

If anyone thinks that there is Self-hood of the intellect and such, in opposition to them, it is further said (literally, an untranslatable interjection signifying reproof or emphasis):

Separated from the mind, eye, and others, that which, by itself,
Is the Mind, Eye, and Others of the mind, eye, and others,
And is of a nature beyond the reach of the mind, eye, and others,
That which by its nature is eternal Knowledge am I, the Self. (5)

"From the mind, eye, and others" is from the mind and such and from the eye and such; "separated from" is being apart from or different from; "that which" is that "I" is the Self (He am I, the Self); thus is the connection.

By the appropriation to oneself, the cause, of the mind, eye, and such, being included in that, also, is the body; this is to be investigated and considered to be included and appropriated.

Because of this, from the body, also, it is separated; thus it is considered and understood.

Therefore, the Guru also says, "From the intellect, the senses, [and] the body, the Self is different. It is omnipresent (all-pervading, eternal) and immovable (constant, unchangeable). The Self shines in and as different forms, at every place, in [all] modes."

"How is this illuminating Self related or connected to the illuminator of the mind, eye, and others? How is it separate from the mind, eye, and others?" Thus approaching, it is replied:

"By itself."

The Self, which, by itself is "the Mind, Eye, and Others of the mind, eye, and others" is the illuminator-mind-eye-and-others of the illumining mind, eye, and others. It is from union with the quality of being illuminating. This is the meaning. Just as the illuminator of the external pot and others, which are the mind, eye, and others, is considered different and reaches far beyond (surpasses), so, likewise, internally, of the mind, eye, and others, the illuminator is the Self that, consequently, reaches far beyond (surpasses) and is different from them. Thus it is ascertained.

Therefore, it is thus established that the mind, eye, and others are of the nature of the non-Self. Other than the known (the to-be-known) is the knower.

"Is it not that, for the Self, also, being the known (the to-be-known), non-Self-hood is applicable?" To that, it is further said:

"Of the nature beyond the reach of the mind, eye, and others," is the self-existent, innate illumination.

Therefore, also, the Sruti (Vedas) says, "from where speech, along with mind, return, unable to reach."

"Then, if the Self is beyond the reach of the mind, eye, and others, how is it, then, to be attained?"

"A pot, cloth, and others are certainly considered (seen) to be dependent on the mind, eye, and others to be established.

"Consequently, for the Self, also, that dependent establishment, or attainment, is connected and is suitable. If that dependent attainment does not exist, is not attained by them, the attainment, indeed, will never be, like a rabbit's horn." To this, it is now said:

That which, being One, the pure Consciousness, though of the nature of the self-luminous,
Shines as if variegated in the minds,
Just as the sun, being one, existing in water in platters,
That which by its nature is eternal Knowledge am I, the Self. (6)

"Which" tells us about being self-accomplished. "One" is without a second. "Shines" is exceedingly shines or illuminates. "By oneself" or "by itself" is on its own alone and not by another. "Pure" is blemishless. "Mind" or "consciousness" or "intelligence" is mind, of which it is one whose "mind is pure" by itself. For the pure-minded, certainly, the Self by itself alone shines, or manifests. Thus is the meaning.

Because of this, indeed, purity of sattva (goodness, of the nature of the true) is the meaning in the Vedas, also, in the repetition and sacred doctrine of the Veda and supplementary statements in accordance with Vedic texts. It is said (lit., prescribed), "It is this here, by the sacred doctrine, with the recitation of the Vedas, that the brahmins wish to inquire about and know by ritual sacrifice (worship), by giving charity, by tapas (austerity, fiery practice), and by fasting."

A pot, cloth, and others, because of inertness and because of dependance upon another illumination [to be perceived], do not shine or manifest [on their own]; it is thus established.

The Self, though, because of being illuminative by its own nature and not dependent upon another illumination, shines like the sun. Just as the sun is self-luminous and does not depend upon another illumination, but certainly shines, likewise the Self, also. Thus is the conviction.

Thus, with the nondual Self-Knowledge arisen, the liberated in life (jīvanmukta), "though of the nature of being self-luminous" truly, being the self-luminous nature of the supreme Truth, "shines variously" in parts, in divisions, "in minds" or in intellects, in the limitations that are mere appearances. That which shines as if various, "That is I, the Self." Thus is the connection.

"Existing in the water in shallow platters," in the conditions abiding, "the sun," the sun, the celestial luminary, though luminous of its own nature, "being one" alone, shines as if various. Like that is the Self, also. This is the purport.

How is there not the liberated in life (jīvanmukta)? (or: How, surely, is there the jīvanmukta?) As long as one is embodied, he is said to be a jīva, or living being. Of him who is living, though, if nonexistence of the body is considered liberation, that is not arrived at, and does not happen, because of contradiction and incompatibility.

Not, indeed, for the living does the nonexistence of the body arise or exist.

Now, certainly, if, being still in the body, cutting asunder, or discontinuance, of enjoyment and experience is liberation, that also is not four-cornered (i.e., incorrect).

As the cause or instrument for all enjoyment and experience is in the possession of the senses, the cutting asunder, or discontinuance, of the enjoyment and experience is impossible.

"The bondage of false, illusory knowledge is, indeed, experience. The cessation of that by true Knowledge is also the discontinuance of experience." If this is so; no, because of the continuance of the onset, the arrival at and assenting to, of the contradictory, absurd, false knowledge, indeed, like the knowledge of two moons and such.

Otherwise, the embodied, indeed, will not be.

Hence, indeed, the wise, such as Janaka and others, being rulers is heard of.

Sruti (the Vedas), also, denies the discontinuance of the enjoyment, or experience, of the embodied, "Verily, of one with a body there is no removing of the existing of (the happening of) the pleasant and unpleasant (likes and dislikes).

"Therefore, unreasonable is jīvanmukti (liberation in life)."

So, it is said that only for the living Knowledge of the Truth arises, but not for the dead. Tranquillity (equanimity, śama), self-control (dama), and such and listening, reflection, and such of the means to Knowledge are impossible for the dead.

Hence, indeed, certainly, the renunciation (saṁnyāsa) of the wise, Yajnavalkya and others, is heard of.

The renunciation of the dead is neither heard of nor exists (happens).

Therefore, for the living (jīvataḥ) the Knowledge of the Truth arises; thus it is established.

Due to Self-Knowledge alone is Liberation; thus accomplished, and established, is jīvanmukti (Liberation in life); "Verily, one who certainly knows that Supreme Brahman himself becomes Brahman; (Verily, one who certainly knows that Supreme Brahman becomes Brahman alone;)" and "The knower of Brahman attains the Supreme," thus and such by (from) the Sruti (Vedas).

"Is it not that liberation is the result of knowledge assisted by, or acting together equally with, another practice, [as indicated] in the Sruti (Vedas)?" If [this is the view], no, because only Knowledge is heard thus, "the knot of the heart is destroyed (split);" "there exists no other path (way) for going ahead (progress, going to the place of refuge);" thus is the negation (denial, disallowance) of "with another practice," also.

Is it not the Sruti (Vedas), indeed, that shows liberation is due to knowledge acting (co-operating) with death as in "of him only as long as, after a delay of a long time, just so long he is not liberated; then it will occur arrive"? No, because of the earlier arising and existence of the knowledge, the state engaged in brought about for a long time, and the inability to make its presence and be made manifest [only] at the time of death.

If [the view is that], "at that moment of time, indeed, liberation is due to the arising or production of other knowledge," it is not so, [for] "What, indeed, Bhagavan knows, that, indeed, tell to me," [and] "The person who has an (ācāryavān) a spiritual teacher knows." Thus, that Liberation is due only to preceding (earlier) knowledge alone is heard of and considered in the original Sruti (Vedas).

By this, another statement becomes accepted and favored: "While alive, indeed, the wise one is certainly liberated from both joy and sorrow, pleasure and pain."

It is not also that such other statements in the Vedas as "Assuredly, there is no destruction of like and dislike of (for) one who is with (in) a body," are contradictory, incompatible, or incongruous, because such other statements in the Vedas pertain to general, universal matters, and here there is special distinction indicated by "the wise."

"Of him only as long": perhaps this Sruti (Vedic statement) should be abandoned. If [that is the view], no, it is a determined, ascertained, established conclusion.

Therefore, indeed, liberation is truly, certainly belonging to one's own nature, and, natural in and for all; it does not originate or arise by knowledge.

So, what then?

In Liberation from the concealment by the darkness of ignorance, only the darkness is removed.

That, also, was removed by the earlier, prior knowledge.

Even so, due to the non-destruction of the body, which is the effect of nescience, again and again, as the great, thick, spiritual darkness that has been driven away, it still conceals.

From the destruction or cessation of the body, there comes about the destruction or cessation of the illusory effect of the concealment.

While this is so, indeed, the preceding removal of the great, thick, spiritual darkness remains dependent only on knowledge, just as, by the sunrise, the removal of the great darkness is done, though the appearance of darkness created by an umbrella and such ceases only upon the cessation, or removal, of the umbrella and such.

Thereupon, also, indeed, the preceding, earlier removal of the great darkness thus remains dependent on the sunrise.

Therefore, there is no liberation from other knowledge (and there is no liberation from different-from-knowledge).

Also, certainly, from knowledge arisen and existent before alone is Liberation. Thus it is established.

Now, if it is that the nondual is the supreme Truth, and false, illusory knowledge expands as the manifested universe (manifestation), if the meaning of the Sruti (Vedas) is thus applied, how is it that there exists, though in opposition or contradiction, the continuance of the manifest universe (manifestation); certainly, is it not, indeed, that, in the ignorance regarding the oyster shell, the manifestation of "silver" and such follows? It is said, "Not thus, not thus, indeed, not from this, thus, there is nothing else higher than not thus," "not here is there variety at all," and such statements being accompanied by "That you are," and such statements; by means of the dissolution of the manifestation (the universe), undoubted and uncontradicted, unrefuted, unobstructed, and unopposed, from that, the nondual Knowledge arises and comes forth.

And it is not proved, or appropriate reasoning, that by the manifestation-conception, or belief, it is contradicted; by complete dissolution, indeed, it arises.

It is again said, how does it follow according to the condition of the belief, or conception, of the manifestation, the expansion of the universe? In this respect, here, it is declared that a twofold hinderance, or opposition, exists. Just as, [appearing] as true, with illusory, false knowledge being the cause, having existed because of bile (jaundice), even in a waking state, a conch [shell] is perceived as yellowish, thus, in knowledge from another cause, there is the perception that this is not yellow, when the causes of the false, illusory knowledge vanish; or just as of weak, foolish vision is the origin, or the cause, of existence of the knowledge of the silver in an oyster shell (nacre), and the knowledge, upon the strong, vision (seeing), that this is not silver; likewise, here, also, as "a yellow conch" is the hindrance, or opposition, to knowledge, [so regarded] as true, in false, illusory knowledge, is the cause, existing in the body, of the belief in a manifested universe contradicted when nondual Knowledge arises.

Therefore, though contradicted as absurd by being its own cause, the knowledge of the manifested universe, like the knowledge of a yellow conch, is born, or produced, again and again.

Certainly, is it not, the body's also being within the manifested universe, destruction, indeed, results and is the consequence. If thus is [the view], no, because of, the continued course or continued influence of prarabdha-karma (karma that has come to fruition).

Like a potter's wheel spinning, because of the samskara (propensity, tendency, mental impression) of the karmas to continue course, or their continued influence, thus liberation in life is attained.

And [if] the destruction of the propensity of karma is only upon the fall of the body, there should also be the complete dissolution of all belief in a manifested universe.

Also, because of the destruction of the other karmas by knowledge, another body does not arise; thus there is supreme liberation.

Also, while thus it is so, by the explanation that knowledge alone is entirely the cause of the attainment of liberation, that action being a cause of liberation is discarded is to be understood.

Just so, certainly, liberation by karma (action) alone is not heard of.

Then, indeed, also, [liberation] because of [action] along with knowledge is, indeed, unheard of.

Is it not that the knowledge and action being together is heard of, [as in] "that knowledge and action held together and pre-existing (prior) knowledge"? [This is] true, but the sphere and scope, the subject, of samsara and that listening, or learning, are not the sphere, scope, or subject of liberation.

If it is said it is the conjoining, or collection, of the meaning (purpose or aim) of the knowledge of impelling directives for the unobtained regarding daily, obligatory and occasional, special purpose karmas (actions, rites) as in "As long as life is, he maintains and gives oblation to the sacred fire in sacrificial ceremonies," and such, no, because there is no proof of the use of these.

"He that by this reading (recitation) of the Vedas the Brahmana-s (Brahmins) seek to know by ritual sacrifice (yajñena), by gifts (charity), by indestructible tapas," in this respect, here, then, is the third [statement of] the Sruti (Vedas) for a use; if [such is the view,] no, "seek to know" is unrelated because of being the aim, or purpose, of the knowledge of the karmas is clearly recognized, and the aim, or purpose, being liberation is not to be conceived, or construed, thus.

Moreover, certainly, Knowledge does not look for assistance in the cessation of ignorance, as from the arising of that (knowledge), indeed, is the inevitable cessation of ignorance.

Therefore, also, the Sruti (the Vedic statement)—"Having known Him alone, he transcends death; there exists no other path for a way (place of refuge)."

Also, if the fruit of action, the result of karma, is liberation, then non-eternality is applicable, like pots and such and like heaven and such.

That, indeed, is the meaning of the Sruti (Vedas) also, aha (indicates command or reproof) "that just as if here the world of accumulated action (karma) is destroyed, thus, indeed, there in the other world, the world of accumulated merit is destroyed."

"Oblation to fire and such, indeed, are for that action (to be done) alone;" thus by the sutra-weaver (author) traditional actions, like the preliminary offering (prayāja) and such, are [precluded from] being the cause of liberation is declared.

Then, there is, with the meaning, purpose, or aim of knowledge, the use of action, indeed.

The arising, or producing, of Knowledge is beyond the use, or employment, of actions, though there is the purpose of the welfare of the world, and acting accordingly in conformity with that, is that which ought to be done. Thus, all is consistent and correct.

Indeed, how can the Self, being one alone, simultaneously govern numerous intellects?

Certainly not is it that one horseman is found to simultaneously control numerous horses.

Control, or governance, though, by sequence is appropriate (logical).

Here, that also is not, because all intellects, indeed, are seen to simultaneously engage in their own respective activities.

Also, there is the impossibility of activity without being directed (governed).

Then, "the Self is not one." Aha (indicates reproof):

Just as the sun, illumining numerous eyes,
Does not illumine sequentially what is to be illumined,
So it is with that which, being One, is the awakener of numerous minds simultaneously,
That which by its nature is eternal Knowledge am I, the Self. (7)

"Just as," by which, being luminous, illuminative by nature, "the sun," the sun, the celestial luminary is one only, "of numerous eyes the illumination (illuminator)" simultaneously governs, or controls, numerous eyes and not "sequentially," not one by one, in the eyes, "illumines that which is to be illuminated," "likewise," in the same way, in that manner, indeed, in that way, "one" and that "awakener" is "being one and being the awakener," that which controls, that governing power, "simultaneously" acts upon, or governs, numerous "minds," intellects, simultaneously governs, not one by one sequentially, not one mind after another, illumines that which is to be illumined "that which is so," that is "I," the Self; thus it is to be connected.

Indeed, if this be so, the sun, itself, is the stimulator of, or the one who sets in motion, the intellect; it is the power behind. How does the Self come in then? There is also the Vedic pronouncement (the Sruti) [says], dhiyo yo naḥ pracodayāt, "he who actuates (impels) our intellect." [The author] continues then:

Just as, illumined by the sun, the eye recognizes the form not illumined,
So, likewise, the One, illumined by which
The sun illumines the eye;
That which by its nature is eternal Knowledge am I, the Self. (8)

"By the sun," by the celestial luminary, "illumined," revealed, or made clear, "form" "just as," the way in which, "the eye," the organ of sight, "grasps or takes in," knows very well and thoroughly "the unillumined," that which is not revealed, like a pot and others that are not revealed in the dark, "likewise," in this way, "the sun" also, "the One," "just so," in the same way, similarly, "revealed by which," established by which, "illumines," reveals, or governs, "the eye." Just as the sun is the governing power, or abode, likewise, that which is the governing power, or abode, of the sun, also, is "I," (He I am), the Self. Thus it is to be connected.

And that "I" is the establisher, governing power of the intellects.

In the Vedas, of course, keeping in view, and intending, the power governing the eye, the stimulation and setting in motion, or impelling, of the intellect by the sun is spoken of, because the eye, empowered and governed by the sun, generates and brings forth the rise of the intellect.

Or, keeping in view the true nature of the Self as the governing power, therefore, it has been said, also,

"The sun, the Self, is the foundation of the universe, too."

Indeed, then should it not, in turn, be established and governed by some other illumination? No, it is not so, because of its self-luminescence, by such words of the Vedas (Sruti) as "there is no other seer," and by such other negations.

Besides,

Just as the sun, the one, in many waters moving
and stationary,
Is to be looked upon as of a nature not following,
Though only One, seen as many in moving minds,
That which by its nature is eternal Knowledge am I,
the Self. (9)

"Just as," in which manner, "the sun," the celestial luminary, "the one," "in waters," in reservoirs, "in those moving as well as stationary," though appearing varied, being the "only one," it shines "ananvag-vibhāvya-svarūpaḥ," that is, "anu" following behind goes (añcati), and thus "anvak" means follows, goes, moves toward, and thus "an-anvak" being the negation of the above, i.e., not following in the wake of, thus is the explanation. That is the one which is to be looked upon as of a nature not following in the wake of; the idea thus expressed is the make-up of the negative compound.

Thus, the meaning comes to be: the sun does not follow into the waters.

What then? Likewise, the sun intensely shining in the sky is erroneously perceived to be in the waters. This is the meaning.

Thus, the one Self alone, being of "the nature that does not follow" in the wake of, does not follow the intellect, the changing divided minds, and the intellects of various beings, though many.

What then? That which, indeed, shines separately by itself, that is "I," the Self. This is the meaning.

Besides,

Just as a great fool with his vision obscured by the clouds
Thinks that the sun obscured by the clouds is not shining,
Likewise, that which seems to be bound to the perception of the ignorant,
That which by its nature is eternal Knowledge am I, the Self. (10)

"By the cloud (ghanena)," by the cloud (meghena), "obscured," veiled, "vision" (dṛṣṭiḥ), seeing (darśanam), he of whom, one with "cloud-obstructed vision," the person, the "cloud-obscured," "the sun," the luminary in the sky, because of the manner of, or just as by which, cloud-covering, "thinks," imagines to be "not shining," without luster, as if of a nature devoid of luminescence or the like.

The ignorant person, one with clouded intellect, because of looking through a cloud-covering, thinks that the sun, though of a luminous nature, is without radiance. Because of this, he is called "highly ignorant" (atimūḍhaḥ).

Due to great ignorance, without taking into consideration the obstruction of his own vision, he thinks of the sun, indeed, as lusterless, non-luminous. The word "and," "also," is for completing the meter.

"Likewise," in that manner, the vision obscured by ignorance (avidyā), understanding, or grasping, the intellect to be the Self and superimposing upon the Self the sorrows and others arising therefrom (from the intellect), "that which shows itself as if bound," "to the vision of the highly ignorant," that is "I," the Self ("He am I, the Self,")—thus it is to be connected.

Besides,

Woven together in all manifest things, the One,
Whom all manifest things do not touch,
Of a nature ever pure and transparent like space,
That which by its nature is eternal Knowledge am I,
the Self. (11)

"In all," without exception, "in manifest things," in the nature of the manifest (quintuplicated) universe, "woven together" by the Reality, the Self, knit together, pervasive everywhere, "the One" alone, all the various things, the multifarious things that are in the manifest world, "whom," the nature of Reality "they do not touch."

How? "Like the sky," like space, "always," at all times, "pure," blemishless, devoid of attachment and other disqualifications or faults, "of a transparent (clear, not shaded) nature" of the nature of the eternal (immortal), that which is the Supreme Brahman, that Self, I am. Thus it is to be connected.

The meaning of what has been discussed, the author sums up.

Just as there is difference for pure crystals due to
conditioning, (apparent limitation, appearance of
another thing),
Likewise there is difference for you in different intellects;
Just as for moons in waters, there is movement to and fro,
Likewise is there movement for you also here (in minds),
O All-pervasive One (Vishnu) (12)

"If there is conditioning," if there is a connection to different conditionings, "in the manner in which there is difference," "bheda, difference," is itself "bhedata, differentiation," (the suffix ta is applied according to grammatical rules,), "of good gems," of the pure stones (jewels), crystals, and others, differentiation due to difference of colors such as red, black, and others, is difference, "likewise," "in regard to differences of intellect," in various intellects, "for you also," Oh Vishnu! there is difference for you also; being the supreme Truth, indeed, your difference, composed of the intellect limiting adjunct, is not, indeed, found. Thus is the meaning.

"Just as in the case of moonlights (candrikāṇām)," moons (candraḥ) are themselves moonlights (candrikāḥ), the suffix ka being used according to grammatical rules, in the pure waters, because of the "unsteadiness of the waters" in which the forms of the reflections are seen; unsteadiness is a conditioning (limiting adjunct), not the reality, "in like manner," because of the unsteadiness of the intellects, "for you also there is unsteadiness," which is a conditioning, or limiting adjunct, and not the absolute Reality, "here," in the intellects, "Oh, Vishnu!" having the character (nature) of being all-pervasive.

Thus concludes the commentary on the *Hastamalakiyam* composed by Sri Sankara Bhagavan, the disciple of Sri Govinda-Bhagavat-pada, the Acarya whose revered feet are worthy of worship, a wandering recluse (mendicant), a realized soul (highest renounced one).

www.ingramcontent.com/pod-product-compliance
Lightning Source LLC
Chambersburg PA
CBHW050608300426
44112CB00013B/2124
* 9 7 8 0 9 8 1 9 4 0 9 9 1 *